Dear Friends,

Deep within each of us lies the voice of our intuitive wisdom. We are all born with intuition, but most of us learn at an early age to discount and ignore it.

In many cultures, including those of most of the indigenous peoples of the world, intuition is acknowledged, respected, and honored as a natural and important aspect of life. Every moment of daily life is guided by a strong sense of connection to the universal life force.

Our modern Western culture, on the other hand, rarely acknowledges the validity or even the existence of intuition. We honor and develop the rational aspect of our nature, and at least until recently, have mostly disregarded the intuitive side.

Fortunately, this is beginning to change. People in all professions and walks of life are recognizing the valuable role that intuition can play in their lives. With a little practice, almost all of us can reclaim and develop our natural intuitive abilities.

By learning to recognize and pay attention to our intuitive feelings, we can access the part of us that knows what is right and true for us at any given moment. As we develop the ability to follow our intuition step-by-step, it can become a powerful guiding force, showing us how to live in ever more creative, alive, and fulfilling ways.

I hope that this journal will be a useful and inspiring tool to help you track your own intuitive journey.

With love,

Shakti Gawain

Dear Friends,

Deep within each of us lies the voice of our intuitive wisdom. We are all born with intuition, but most of us learn at an early age to discount and ignore it. In many cultures, including those of most of the indigenous peoples of the world, intuition is acknowledged, respected, and honored as a natural and important aspect of life. Every moment of daily life is guided by a strong sense of connection to the universal life force.

Our modern Western culture, on the other hand, rarely acknowledges the validity or even the existence of intuition. We honor and develop the rational aspect of our nature, and at least until recently, have mostly disregarded the intuitive side. Fortunately, this is beginning to change. People in all professions and walks of life are recognizing the valuable role that intuition can play in their lives. With a little practice, almost all of us can reclaim and develop our natural intuitive abilities. By learning to recognize and pay attention to our intuitive feelings, we can access the part of us that knows what is right and true for us at any given moment. As we develop the ability to follow our intuition step-by-step, it can become a powerful guiding force, showing us how to live in ever more creative, alive, and fulfilling ways.

I hope that this journal will be a useful and inspiring tool to help you track your own intuitive journey.

With love,

WHEN YOU'RE ANXIOUS OR UPSET,

GIVE THAT FEELING A VOICE.

BE SYMPATHETIC AND SUPPORTIVE

AND ASK THE FEELING TO TELL YOU

WHAT'S GOING ON AND HOW YOU CAN

BEST CARE FOR YOURSELF.

FOLLOWING MY INNER GUIDANCE PUTS ME IN SYNC WITH THE UNIVERSE.
I BECOME PHYSICALLY HEALTHIER AND MORE VITAL, MENTALLY CLEARER
AND MORE RELAXED, AND EMOTIONALLY AND SPIRITUALLY FULFILLED.

OUR INTUITIVE GUIDANCE
IS ENLIVENING. IT BRINGS FEELINGS
OF OPENNESS, RELIEF, AND RELEASE.
IT FEELS GOOD IN OUR HEART
AND SOUL, SHOWING US EXACTLY
THE RIGHT STEP TO TAKE.

My intuition is always trying

to help me be more of

who I am by fully expressing

my power, truth, and creativity,

and by

loving and trusting

myself completely.

MY INTUITION IS ALWAYS TRYING

TO HELP ME BE MORE OF

WHO I AM BY FULLY EXPRESSING

MY POWER, TRUTH, AND CREATIVITY,

AND BY

LOVING AND TRUSTING

MYSELF COMPLETELY.

Notice what's on your mind right now and pay attention to those things your mind keeps coming back to. Be aware of how your body feels. Is there something you need to pay attention to or take action on?

I GIVE MYSELF PERMISSION TO FOLLOW INTUITIVE IMPULSES AND SEE WHAT HAPPENS. SOMETHING WITHIN MAY BE TRYING TO COME THROUGH; EXCITING NEW DOORS MAY BE READY TO OPEN.

I IMAGINE THAT I HAVE A WISE BEING
LIVING WITHIN MYSELF. I CAN TALK TO IT,
MAKE REQUESTS, AND EVEN ASK QUESTIONS.
AS I DO SO, I REMAIN OPEN TO THE
ANSWERS. THEY ARE USUALLY VERY SIMPLE
AND FEEL PROFOUNDLY RIGHT.

THE MORE I FOLLOW MY

INNER WISDOM,

THE BETTER I AM ABLE

TO CARE FOR MYSELF

AND THE MORE THINGS

JUST FALL INTO PLACE.

THE MORE I FOLLOW MY

INNER WISDOM,

THE BETTER I AM ABLE

TO CARE FOR MYSELF

AND THE MORE THINGS

JUST FALL INTO PLACE.

WHEN I ALLOW MYSELF
TO BE GUIDED, IT DOESN'T MEAN
THAT I WON'T MAKE MISTAKES OR HAVE
FAILURES. I AM WILLING TO LET
THINGS THAT AREN'T WORKING GO
AND PURSUE WHAT IS WORKING.

GETTING IN TOUCH
WITH MY INTUITION
UNBLOCKS MY CREATIVITY
AND PUTS ME IN THE FLOW —
MY MOST ALIVE AND
PRODUCTIVE STATE.

Conduct an experiment.
Pick a period of time such as
a day or a week. During that time,
allow yourself to believe that
you are 100 percent right in
whatever you intuitively feel —
and act accordingly.

INNER GUIDANCE CAN COME IN THE

FORM OF WORDS, MENTAL IMAGES,

OR FEELING IMPRESSIONS.

YOU MAY ALSO FEEL

A RADIANT WARMTH,

OR SENSE ENERGY

FLOWING THROUGH YOU.

INNER GUIDANCE CAN COME IN THE

FORM OF WORDS, MENTAL IMAGES,

OR FEELING IMPRESSIONS.

YOU MAY ALSO FEEL

A RADIANT WARMTH,

OR SENSE ENERGY

FLOWING THROUGH YOU.

Help yourself remember to tune into your intuition by putting visual reminders around your home or work area. You might use notes, poems, pictures, or any object that conveys a feeling of inner connection.

TRUSTING MY INTUITION ISN'T SELFISH, IRRESPONSIBLE, OR
INCONSIDERATE OF OTHERS. SINCE INTUITION IS CONNECTED TO THE UNIVERSAL
INTELLIGENCE, HEEDING IT ALWAYS LEADS TO THE GREATEST GOOD FOR ALL.

I IMAGINE THAT I HAVE A WISE BEING

LIVING WITHIN MYSELF.

I CAN TALK TO IT,

MAKE REQUESTS, AND EVEN ASK QUESTIONS.

AS I DO SO, I REMAIN OPEN TO THE ANSWERS.

THEY ARE USUALLY VERY SIMPLE

AND FEEL PROFOUNDLY RIGHT.

Ask yourself,

"What do i most need to remember

or be aware of right now?"

Be quiet for a moment

and sense the answer

coming from within you.

ASK YOURSELF,

"WHAT DO I MOST NEED TO REMEMBER

OR BE AWARE OF RIGHT NOW?"

BE QUIET FOR A MOMENT

AND SENSE THE ANSWER

COMING FROM WITHIN YOU.

MAKE A LIST OF THE CAREER OR
CREATIVITY FANTASIES YOU'VE HAD.
BESIDE THAT LIST,
MAKE ANOTHER THAT DETAILS THE
CONCRETE ACTION STEPS YOU CAN TAKE
TO EXPLORE THOSE FANTASIES.

WHEN I LISTEN TO IT,

MY INTUITION CAN SHOW ME

STEP BY STEP WHAT I NEED TO DO

TO FULFILL MY DEEPEST DESIRES

AND ACHIEVE MY GOALS.

CHECKING IN WITH YOURSELF
EACH DAY CAN BE EXTREMELY POWERFUL.
YOU DON'T NEED MUCH TIME. WITH
PRACTICE, YOU CAN LEARN TO QUICKLY
AND EASILY DROP OUT OF YOUR MIND
AND INTO A DEEPER PLACE INSIDE.

RELAX,

LET GO, AND LISTEN

A LITTLE MORE DEEPLY THAN USUAL.

DON'T TRY TO

MAKE SOMETHING HAPPEN;

ALLOW IT TO HAPPEN.

RELAX.

LET GO, AND LISTEN

A LITTLE MORE DEEPLY THAN USUAL.

DON'T TRY TO

MAKE SOMETHING HAPPEN;

ALLOW IT TO HAPPEN.

THERE IS A UNIVERSAL,
INTELLIGENT LIFE FORCE WITHIN
EVERYONE AND EVERYTHING. IT RESIDES
IN EACH OF US AS A DEEP WISDOM,
AN INNER KNOWING.

DESCRIBE YOUR IDEAL SCENE — YOUR "DREAM" JOB, HOME,
OR YOUR LIFE AS YOU WOULD LIKE IT TO BE. WRITE THIS DOWN IN
THE PRESENT TENSE, AS THOUGH IT WERE ALREADY TRUE, AND LET YOURSELF
ENJOY THE FEELING OF HAVING WHAT YOU WANT.

REMEMBER A TIME WHEN YOU HAD

A STRONG HUNCH OR "GUT FEELING."

HOW DID IT FEEL?

DID YOU FOLLOW IT?

WHAT HAPPENED WHEN

YOU DID OR DID NOT?

I VISUALIZE MYSELF FEELING,

TRUSTING, AND FOLLOWING

MY OWN ENERGY. I AM COMPLETELY

TRUE TO MYSELF, ALIVE AND

EMPOWERED, FULLY AND

FREELY CREATIVE.

I VISUALIZE MYSELF FEELING,

TRUSTING, AND FOLLOWING

MY OWN ENERGY. I AM COMPLETELY

TRUE TO MYSELF, ALIVE AND

EMPOWERED, FULLY AND

FREELY CREATIVE.

WE ARE ALL BORN WITH INTUITION,
BUT IT IS OFTEN TRAINED OUT OF US
EARLY IN LIFE. WITH PRACTICE,
WE CAN GET BACK IN TOUCH WITH IT
AND ALLOW IT TO GUIDE US.

THE THINGS THAT AREN'T WORKING
IN MY LIFE ARE OPPORTUNITIES
FOR LEARNING. THEY REFLECT OLD
PATTERNS THAT NEED MY AWARENESS,
ATTENTION, AND HEALING. AS I DO THAT
INNER WORK, THINGS WILL START
TO SHIFT IN MY LIFE.

INTUITION ISN'T AUTHORITARIAN
OR JUDGMENTAL. IT NEVER FEELS HEAVY
OR BURDENSOME, DOESN'T MAKE
US FEEL GUILTY, AND NEVER LEADS US
TO DO ANYTHING THAT ISN'T PHYSICALLY OR
EMOTIONALLY GOOD FOR US.